A Dollar, a Penny, How Much and How Many?

For Henry Collins Norman
—B.P.C.

Money:
the coins and bills
people use to
buy things

A Dollar, a Penny,

How Much and

How Many?

by Brian P. Cleary

illustrated by Brian Gable

M Millbrook Press / Minneapolis

Money is the term for coins and bills that people use

to buy things such as pizzas,

pencils,

planes,

and chains

and shoes.

U.S. coins are metal, small, and round, while bills are made

of paper, cut rectangular,
with famous folks portrayed.

Common coins are pennies,

nickels,

dimes,

and quarters too,

8

and you'll know
how much each is worth
before this lesson's through.

Pennies each are worth 1 cent.
A nickel is worth 5.

It takes 10 cents to make a dime.
A quarter's 25.

1 dollar's worth of coins can look a lot of different ways.

Let's go inside this dollar store
and see how each cat pays.

13

Jenny brought 4 quarters, while 10 dimes came with her brother.

$1.00

Anna paid 100 pennies (taken from her mother).

Zack hands over 7 dimes,
1 quarter,
plus 5 pennies.

All these combinations prove
to be the same as Jenny's.

Paper money doesn't look or feel like coins at all.

But it can also pay for things, however large or small.

Common bills include the 20,

10,

and 5

and 1.

With special inks,
most green and black,
we print them by the ton.

but there are other ways to pay with different bills. Just look:

four **5**-dollar bills would work.

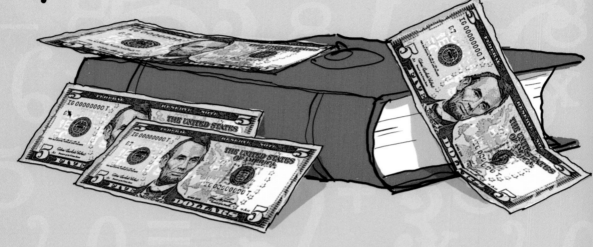

Two **10s** would do it too,

or twenty 1s would pay the funds.
That's just to name a few!

Money is not magical—
it doesn't grow on trees.

It's something you can save or lend or spend on what you please.

27

In back are stacks of money facts, so you'll have me to thank

When you take your knowledge off to class—
or take it to the bank!

U.S. BILLS

$1.00

$5.00

$10.00

$20.00

Find activities, games, and more at
www.brianpcleary.com

ABOUT THE AUTHOR & ILLUSTRATOR

BRIAN P. CLEARY is the author of the best-selling Words Are CATegorical© series as well as the Math Is CATegorical©, Food Is CATegorical™, Animal Groups Are CATegorical™, Adventures in Memory™, and Sounds Like Reading© series. He has also written Do You Know Dewey? Exploring the Dewey Decimal System, Six Sheep Sip Thick Shakes: And Other Tricky Tongue Twisters, and several other books. Mr. Cleary lives in Cleveland, Ohio.

BRIAN GABLE is the illustrator of many Words Are CATegorical© books and the Math Is CATegorical© series. Mr. Gable also works as a political cartoonist for the Globe and Mail newspaper in Toronto, Canada.

Text copyright © 2012 by Brian P. Cleary
Illustrations copyright © 2012 by Lerner Publishing Group, Inc.

Millbrook Press
A division of Lerner Publishing Group, Inc.
241 First Avenue North
Minneapolis, MN 55401 USA

For reading levels and more information,
look up this title at www.lernerbooks.com.

Main body text set in RandumTEMP 35/48. Typeface provided by House Industries.

Library of Congress Cataloging-in-Publication Data

Cleary, Brian P., 1959-
    A dollar, a penny, how much and how many? / by Brian P. Cleary ; illustrated by Brian Gable.
        p.   cm. — (Math is CATegorical)
    ISBN: 978-0-8225-7882-6 (lib. bdg. : alk. paper)
    ISBN: 978-1-4677-0128-0 (eb pdf)
    1. Money—Juvenile literature. 2. Coins—Juvenile literature. I. Gable, Brian, 1949- ill. II. Title.
HG221.5.C54 2012
332.4'973—dc23   2011045864

Manufactured in the United States of America
5-43720-8700-1/20/2017